GOD
Sees Me

FRANKA CHIGBOGWU

WestBow Press books may be ordered through booksellers or by contacting:

WestBow Press
A Division of Thomas Nelson & Zondervan
1663 Liberty Drive
Bloomington, IN 47403
www.westbowpress.com
1 (866) 928-1240

Interior Image Credit: Franka Chigbogwu

ISBN: 978-1-9736-9096-2 (sc)
ISBN: 978-1-9736-9097-9 (e)

Library of Congress Control Number: 2020907723

Print information available on the last page.

WestBow Press rev. date: 5/1/2020

Introduction

to parents

GOD SEES ME This book is right from the heart of God. I was praying one night, at about 3 am, and was asking God what title to give the book He layed in my heart. Spontaneously, came His voice, GOD SEES ME. The Holy Spirit did not stop there. He began telling me word for word what to write on each of the pages of the book. Being someone who always keeps a piece of paper and a pen by the bedside, I quickly picked up my writing material and began to write as fast as I could as the Spirit spoke.

I can say that this book is a special blessing from God to every child as a guard against any type of fear. I believe it would also help parents to remember at the same time as they read with their child/children that no matter where they are, what they are doing, or what is going on in their lives, and in any situation/s, that God sees them all. God does not just see us, He also cares about everything in our lives.

Dedication

This book is dedicated first to The TRINITY (God the Father, God the Son, and God the Holy Spirit) for putting this idea in my heart. I thank Him for granting me grace daily, for life and breath. To my husband, and our precious children: Oge, Nkem, Onyeka and Ify, for their love, care, and encouragement, also for being special blessings in our home. I wouldn't have been able to do this without you all. Lots of LOVE deep from my heart.

God sees me when I am quietly studying.

God sees me in my room when I am all by myself.

God sees me even when I hide under my bed.

God sees me when I am sleeping in the night, all alone in my bed after mom tucks me in.

I'm not really alone because He's right there with me.

God sees me when I am playing hide and seek with my friends.

God sees me when I am sad.

God sees me when I am happy.

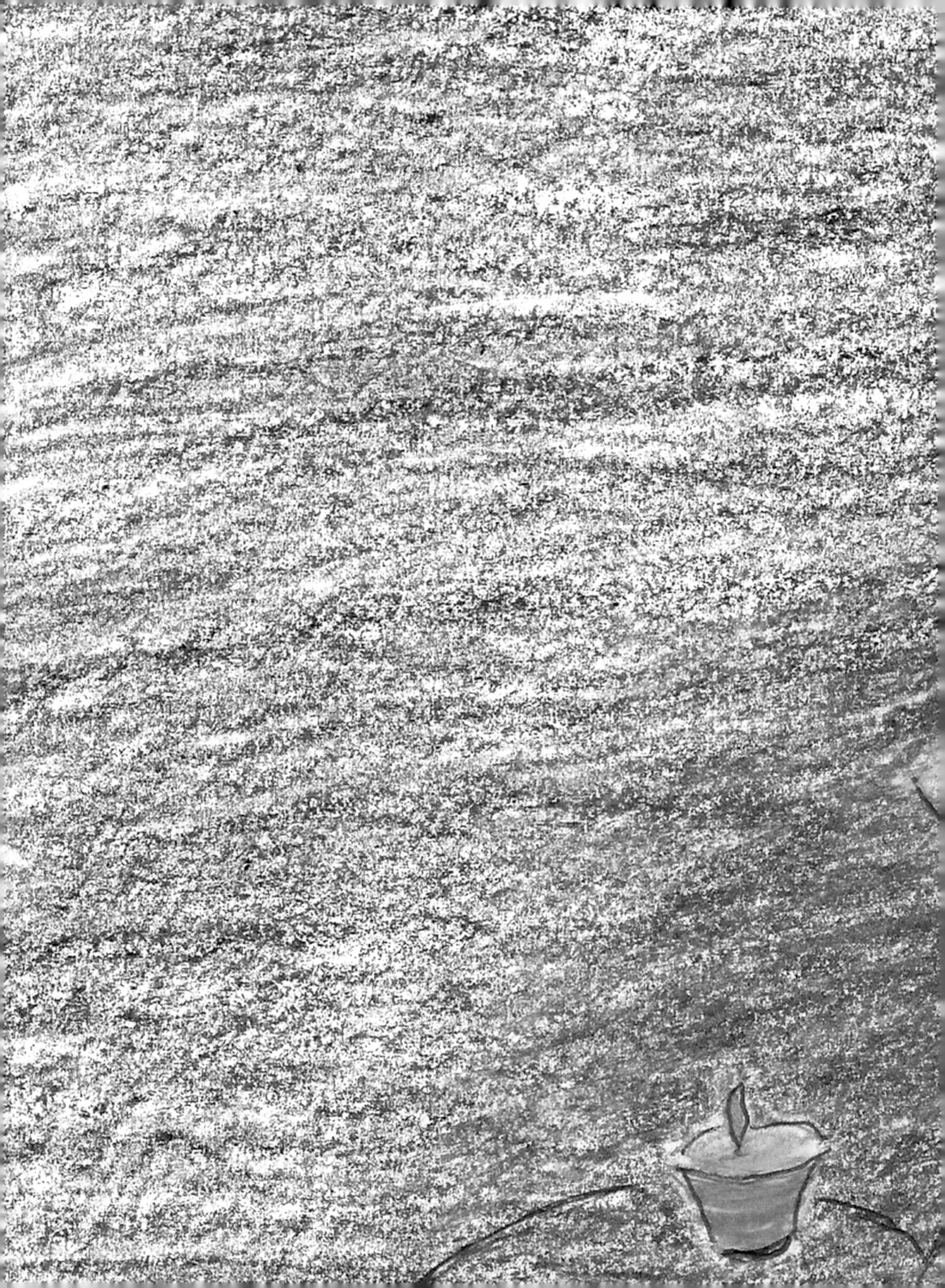

God sees me even in the dark.

God sees me in the light.

God sees me. I cannot hide from Him, He is always with me.

God sees me anywhere. God sees me everywhere. God sees me anytime. God sees me everytime. I am not alone. I am not afraid. He is always watching over me.

He is right here with me. He is right there with you. He made the whole world.

He does not sleep. He does not slumber.

He is The God who sees.

Printed in the United States
By Bookmasters